ENVIRONMENTAL
ISSUES

**Book**Life

By Harriet Brundle

©2018
Book Life
King's Lynn
Norfolk PE30 4LS

ISBN: 978-1-78637-256-7

Written by:
Harriet Brundle

Edited by:
Kirsty Holmes

Designed by:
Danielle Rippengill

A catalogue record for this book
is available from the British Library.

# CONTENTS

Words that look like **this** can be found in the glossary on page 24.

# WHAT IS SUSTAINABILITY?

Most things we need to live, like fresh water, air and food, don't last forever. If we use a bit of something, we need to look after or replace it, so that there will be more to use again. This is called 'sustainability'.

JUST 1% OF WATER ON EARTH IS DRINKABLE. WE NEED TO LOOK AFTER IT.

The things we need to live, such as water, air and materials to build with, are called **natural resources**. It's important to make sure we have enough of these things to support ourselves, and future **generations**.

# WHY IS SUSTAINABLE LIVING IMPORTANT?

Some resources we need are non-renewable. This means they could run out, and there won't be any more. **Fossil fuels**, such as coal and oil, will run out one day. We use these to make power, so we shouldn't waste them.

WE NEED TO FIND OTHER WAYS TO MAKE ENERGY, TOO.

WATER POLLUTION

Other resources are renewable, but we must not ruin them.
If we **pollute** our fresh water, we won't be able to use it anymore.

# YOUR CARBON FOOTPRINT

Your carbon footprint is how much carbon dioxide you release into the air from the energy you use up. Carbon dioxide is a **gas** that can be harmful to the **environment** in large amounts.

Carbon dioxide also creates a thick blanket around the Earth, trapping heat near the planet's **surface**. This means the planet is getting hotter, which is bad for us and the Earth's wildlife.

IT'S IMPORTANT TO CREATE LESS CARBON DIOXIDE WHEN WE CAN.

# REDUCE, REUSE, RECYCLE

Reducing the amount of waste and pollution we create is very important to sustainable living. We should reuse things again and again instead of throwing them away.

THIS SHOPPING BAG CAN BE REUSED.

If something can't be reused then we should recycle it, if we can. This means it will get turned into something new. These plastic bottles can be melted down and made into new ones.

THIS SIGN MEANS SOMETHING CAN BE RECYCLED.

# RECYCLING AT HOME

We can all try to live in a more sustainable way by recycling whatever we can. Waste that can be recycled usually goes in a separate bin at home. Ask your parents how you can help recycle things you can't use again.

Plastic, glass and paper can all be recycled. So can some metal and cloth. See if you can find out what can be recycled where you live.

GLASS

PLASTIC

PAPER

# SWITCH IT OFF

Using light bulbs, heating and other electrical **appliances** at home uses energy. This energy is made by burning fossil fuels. Using less energy at home means less fossil fuels need to be burnt, which will help the environment.

We can try to live more sustainably by making sure we switch things off when we are not using them. Make sure you turn off the lights when you leave a room, and turn the television off when you are done watching it.

# WALK, BIKE, BUS

Cars produce a lot of carbon dioxide. Walk when you can, or use a bike for short journeys.

For long journeys, use public transport like a bus or a train. The more people use public transport, the less cars are on the road. This helps reduce air pollution. Many buses now use **eco-friendly** fuel too!

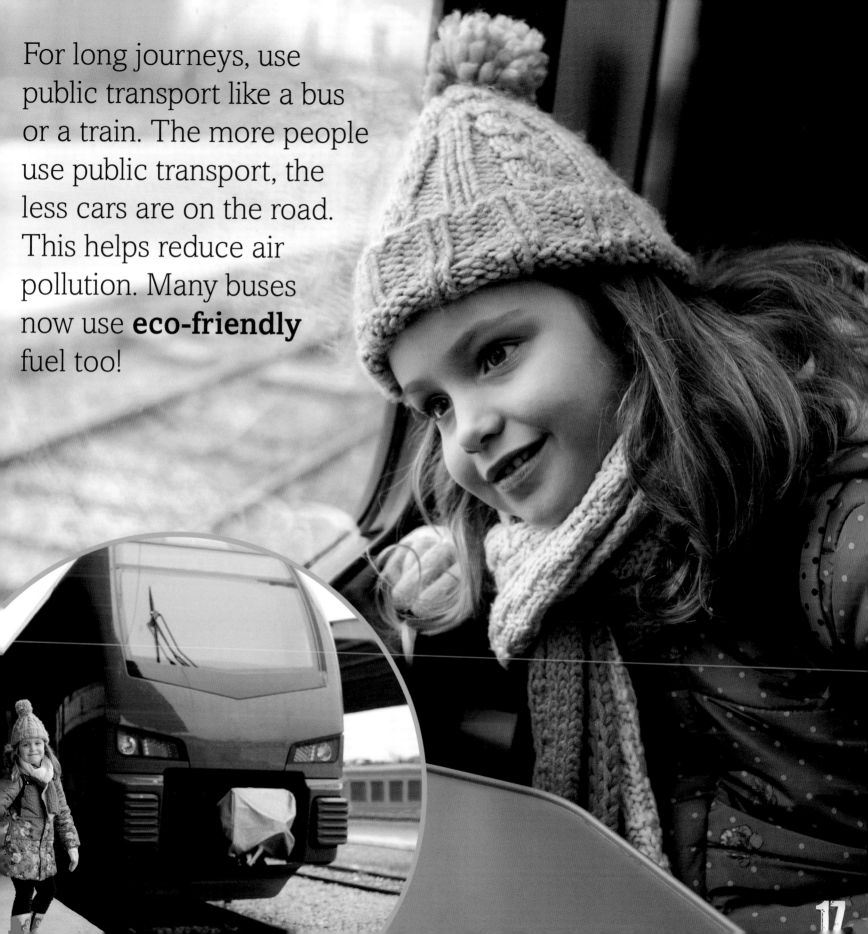

# THINK LOCAL, ACT GLOBAL

When trying to live a sustainable life, it is important to remember to: "Think Local, Act **Global**". This means we can keep our whole planet healthy by taking big or small actions in our local area.

If we all make small changes to live more sustainably – like using less water, growing our own fruit and vegetables or using a bike instead of a car – together we can all help to make a difference to the planet.

# SUSTAINABLE ENERGY

Some resources we need will eventually run out altogether. This means we need to think of new ways to power our cars, houses and factories.

**WIND TURBINES USE WIND TO MAKE ENERGY.**

By using things that will never run out, such as the power of the Sun, we can produce energy without harming the environment.

Buying re-chargeable batteries means they can be used again and again, rather than be thrown away.

A$^{++}$

A$^{++}$

A$^{+}$

A

B

C

D

# WHAT DOES THE FUTURE HOLD?

Countries all around the world are spending money on ways to reduce their carbon footprint and lessen harm to the environment. It is hoped that with new technologies, we can all live a more sustainable lifestyle.

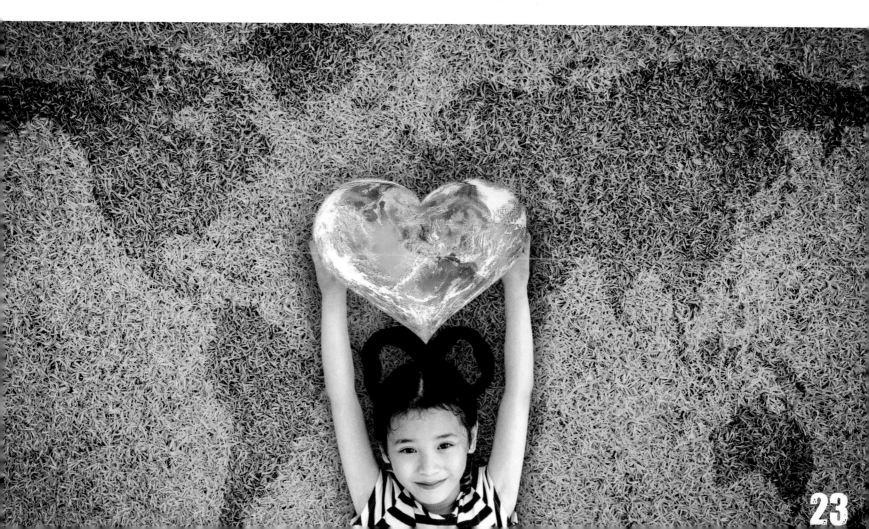

# GLOSSARY

**appliances** pieces of equipment that are made to complete a single task

**eco-friendly** good for the environment

**environment** the natural world

**fossil fuels** fuels, such as coal, oil and gas, that formed millions of years ago from the remains of animals and plants

**gas** air-like substances that freely expand to fill any space available

**generations** groups of people who are roughly the same age

**global** relating to the whole world

**pollute** make poisonous or dirty through the actions of humans

**natural resources** useful materials that are created by nature

**surface** the outer part of something

# INDEX

**Photocredits: Abbreviations: l–left, r–right, b–bottom, t–top, c–centre, m–middle. All images are courtesy of Shutterstock.com.**
Cover – Somchai Som, Digital Genetics, Anan Kaewkhammul. 1 – Mopic. 2 – ampol sonthong. 4 – greenaperture. 5 – Monkey Business Images. 6 – maziarz. 7 – BMJ. 8 – urfin. 9 – Volodymyr Goinyk. 10bl – Mega Pixel, 10r – Rawpixel.com. 11 – FooTToo. 12 – Rawpixel.com. 13l – small smiles, 13m – donatas1205 , 13r – Africa Studio. 14l – gmstockstudio, 14r – Hard Ligth. 15 – andras_csontos. 16 – wavebreakmedia. 17 – maRRitch. 18 – Stepan Kapl. 19 – Gladskikh Tatiana. 20 – Delpixel. 21 – Thinnapob Proongsak. 22m – Delpixel, 22r – Oleksandr Kostiuchenko. 23 – Chinnapong.